"*The battle has not yet been won; we have barely begun.... America has no choice but to do better to assure justice for all Americans, Afro and white, rich and poor, educated and illiterate....Our futures are bound together.*"

—THURGOOD MARSHALL

THURGOOD MARSHALL

BY CARLA WILLIAMS

The Child's World

COVER PHOTO
Portrait of Thurgood Marshall
©Bettmann/Corbis

Published in the United States of America by The Child's World®, Inc.
PO Box 326
Chanhassen, MN 55317-0326
800-599-READ
www.childsworld.com

Product Manager Mary Francis-DeMarois/The Creative Spark
Designer Robert E. Bonaker/Graphic Design & Consulting Co.
Editorial Direction Elizabeth Sirimarco Budd
Contributors Mary Berendes, Red Line Editorial, Katherine Stevenson, Ph.D.

The Child's World®, Inc., and Journey to Freedom® are the sole property
and registered trademarks of The Child's World®, Inc.

Library of Congress Cataloging-in-Publication Data
Williams, Carla, 1965–
Thurgood Marshall / by Carla Williams.
p. cm.
Includes bibliographical references and index.
ISBN 1-56766-924-7
1. Marshall, Thurgood, 1908–1993—Juvenile literature. 2. United
States. Supreme Court—Biography—Juvenile literature.
3. Judges—United States—Biography—Juvenile literature. [1. Marshall,
Thurgood, 1908–1993. 2. Judges. 3. United States. Supreme
Court—Biography. 4. African Americans—Biography. 5. Civil rights
movements—History—20th century.]   I. Title.
KF8745.M34 W55 2002
347.73'2634—dc21
2001000232

Contents

From Troublemaker to Honor Student

Thoroughgood Marshall was born in Baltimore, Maryland, on July 2, 1908. His father, William, was a waiter and a steward. As a steward, William was in charge of the other black workers at his job. At the time, it was a good job for a black man to have. Thoroughgood's mother, Norma, was a schoolteacher. Thoroughgood had one older brother named William Jr., who was called by his middle name, Aubrey.

Norma and William Marshall knew that education was very important for their sons. Norma made sure they went to school. She wanted them to succeed and never let them give up. William had not been able to finish school when he was young. He was always sorry for this because he had wanted to be a lawyer. He liked to **debate** and argue with his sons at dinner. In this way, he taught them to think about what they said. William wanted his sons to be able to speak intelligently about anything. It was an early lesson for Thoroughgood

that would be important later in his life. The dinnertime debates with his father made Thoroughgood want to become a lawyer.

Thoroughgood was named after his grandfather, Thoroughgood "Thorney" Marshall. Thorney was born a slave. The Marshall family liked to tell the story that Thorney was so disobedient, his owner had to set him free. In truth, Thorney escaped from his owner when he was about 14 years old. He then went to live in Baltimore. Many of the black people who lived in there were not slaves. They had escaped, been set free, or otherwise attained their freedom. Thorney worked as a waiter after he escaped. Soon he joined the U.S. Army and went to Texas. When he returned to Baltimore, he opened a grocery store. Thoroughgood was just as independent as Thorney. As a child, he tired of spelling his long name and began to spell it "Thurgood." He even got his mother to change the spelling on his birth certificate. Thurgood's nickname was "Goody."

Bettmann/Corbis

THURGOOD MARSHALL WAS THE FIRST AFRICAN AMERICAN TO BE NAMED TO THE U.S. SUPREME COURT. BUT EVEN BEFORE HE RECEIVED THAT HONOR, HE HAD ACHIEVED GREAT THINGS AS A LAWYER.

Office of the Curator, The Supreme Court of the United States

Thurgood's other grandfather, Isaiah Williams, was born free. Unlike most African Americans at that time, he was never a slave. Isaiah joined the navy and worked for a ship's captain during the Civil War. After the war, Isaiah became a businessman. He owned two grocery stores in Baltimore. Isaiah Williams believed that all people in the United States should have **civil rights.** He knew that all people were equal, no matter what color they were. He often said that black children should be allowed to go to public schools. He did not know that one day his grandson would be the person to make this possible.

Both of Thurgood's grandmothers, Annie Robinson and Mary Fossett, were born free in Baltimore. Both women were lucky because they could read and write. Many black people were not given the chance to learn these skills. In fact, for slaves, learning to read and write was against the law. Thurgood's parents and grandparents believed in equality for everyone. They taught this belief to Thurgood and his brother Aubrey.

The Marshall boys grew up with both black and white neighbors. This was unusual at the time. Most people in the United States were **segregated**—black people lived separately from white people.

As a young boy, Thurgood was the class troublemaker. He did not work at his studies but preferred to read detective stories. Thurgood's school was next door to the police station. He could look out of his classroom window and see the prisoners. He noticed that black people were not treated fairly. In fact, the police often beat them. Thurgood knew this was wrong. He began to think more about becoming a lawyer. He thought that laws should be changed to protect black people.

Thurgood began to work harder in school. He got better grades, but he did not stop playing around. In high school, he was still getting into trouble. To punish him, his teachers made him read the **Constitution** of the United States. Thurgood was in trouble a lot. By the time he graduated from high school, he had learned the whole Constitution by heart!

Moorland Spingarn Research Center

THURGOOD'S MOTHER, NORMA, WAS A SCHOOL-TEACHER. SHE DEMANDED THAT HER SONS STUDY HARD. HER HIGH EXPEC-TATIONS PAID OFF. AUBREY BECAME A SURGEON, AND THURGOOD BECAME A SUCCESSFUL LAWYER AND JUDGE.

IN 1925, THURGOOD POSED WITH OTHER MEMBERS OF HIS FRATERNITY, A COLLEGE CLUB. HE IS SHOWN IN THE MIDDLE ROW, SECOND FROM RIGHT.

Thurgood went to college at Lincoln University in Pennsylvania—the first American university for black students. His brother Aubrey was also a student at Lincoln. Aubrey was studying to become a doctor. The two Marshall boys were quite different. Aubrey was a quiet boy, but Thurgood spoke loudly. Thurgood played cards and read comic books. He watched cowboy movies. He was a popular and fun student at Lincoln.

The Marshalls had protected Aubrey and Thurgood from **racism.** The brothers did not fully realize how unfairly black people were treated. Thurgood did not know just how much some Americans disliked black people. They disliked them so much, they did not want to be near them. A man named Langston Hughes was Thurgood's classmate at Lincoln. Langston was already a famous poet when he went to college. The other students looked up to him. He taught Thurgood a very important lesson.

The students at Lincoln voted on whether to have both white and black teachers. Thurgood and most of the other students voted that they did not want black teachers. Sadly, they believed that whites would be better teachers. But Langston Hughes voted in favor of black teachers. He thought that black students should have black role models. He knew that having teachers who looked like them would make the students feel proud. He also knew that black teachers should have the same chance to teach as white teachers. Langston wrote a school paper to say so. He gave talks to the other students. Thurgood began to agree with Langston. He realized that change could happen if people worked together. The next time there was a vote, Thurgood voted for the black teachers. A black teacher started to work at the school the following year. Thurgood also became more serious about his studies.

In his senior year, Thurgood met 17-year-old Vivian Burey. Her nickname was "Buster." Buster was from Philadelphia. She was a student at the University of Pennsylvania. The couple married in her hometown. They rented a small apartment in Oxford, near Lincoln University. Twenty-year-old Thurgood went back to Lincoln to finish college. He spent even more time studying. The next year, he graduated from college with honors. He began to think about going to law school.

Lawyer and Civil Rights Champ

After graduating from college, Thurgood Marshall moved back to Baltimore. He and his wife lived with his parents. Marshall wanted to go to the University of Maryland Law School, but it did not accept African American students. That made him angry. He knew it was not fair to keep him out just because he was black. At this time, white people and black people were still segregated in many states. They could not live next door to one another. They could not go to school together. In some states, they could not even drink from the same water fountains. The laws and customs that enforced this separation were called "Jim Crow." (Jim Crow was a black character in a **minstrel** show, but no one is sure how the term came to mean segregation.) Many people—including Thurgood Marshall—knew the Jim Crow laws were wrong. They wanted to do away with them for good.

Marshall went to Howard University Law School in Washington, D.C. He took a job in the school's law library. That way, he could study the law even when he was at work. The **Supreme Court** of the United States is also located in Washington, D.C. While he was a law student, Marshall sometimes skipped class. He went to the Supreme Court to listen to the lawyers present their **cases.** He heard some of the best lawyers in the country argue their cases before the Supreme Court. Marshall wanted to become one of those lawyers.

In law school, Marshall met Charles Hamilton Houston. Houston was the new **dean** of the law school. He was a stiff and proper man. Some of the students were afraid of him. He was a tough teacher who wanted only the best work from his students.

Corbis

AFTER GRADUATING FROM LINCOLN UNIVERSITY IN JUNE OF
1930, THURGOOD MARSHALL DECIDED TO STUDY LAW AT
HOWARD UNIVERSITY IN WASHINGTON, D.C. HOWARD, SHOWN
ABOVE, WAS FOUNDED IN 1867 FOR NEWLY FREED SLAVES.

Courtesy of Howard University

CHARLES HAMILTON HOUSTON WAS A RESPECTED
PROFESSOR AT HOWARD UNIVERSITY WHO DEDICATED
HIS CAREER TO THE AFRICAN AMERICAN STRUGGLE
FOR EQUAL RIGHTS. HE INSPIRED THURGOOD
MARSHALL TO USE THE LAW TO FIGHT SEGREGATION.

Houston had been the first African American lawyer to argue a case before the Supreme Court. He taught his students that they would gain civil rights only by changing laws. He believed that segregation went against the U.S. Constitution. He believed in **integration**—in white and black people living and going to school together. Mr. Houston became Marshall's role model. Marshall worked hard in law school. He graduated first in his class, with the best grades of all the students.

In 1933, Marshall earned his law degree and opened his own law office in Baltimore. At that time, people were very poor. It was a period known as the **Great Depression,** when there was little business activity. Many of the people who came to Marshall for help could not pay him. He took their cases anyway. He kept working hard. He soon began to get clients who could pay.

In 1934, Marshall went to work for the National Association for the Advancement of Colored People (NAACP). The NAACP wanted civil rights for all Americans. To achieve this, it needed good lawyers to win cases in court. Thurgood and Buster Marshall moved to New York City for his new job.

It still bothered Marshall that he had not been allowed to attend the University of Maryland Law School. He wanted to take the school to court. He believed the law would prove that segregation was wrong.

In 1936, an African American man **sued** the University of Maryland for refusing to admit him. Marshall and Charles Houston took his case. They argued against segregation and won. The University of Maryland finally agreed to admit African American students. It was a personal and public victory for Marshall. Even though it was too late for him to go to school there, he had made sure that no other black students would be turned away because of their skin color. Marshall's next big case was to make sure that black teachers in Maryland earned the same pay as white teachers. His mother was a teacher. He knew she worked as hard as the white teachers. He won that case, too.

Library of Congress

MARSHALL (LEFT) HAD ONCE HOPED TO STUDY AT THE UNIVERSITY OF MARYLAND LAW SCHOOL, BUT HE WAS NOT ACCEPTED BECAUSE HE WAS BLACK. IN 1936, HE AND CHARLES HOUSTON (RIGHT) TOOK ON AN IMPORTANT CASE. THEY WENT TO COURT TO CHALLENGE THE ALL-WHITE POLICY AT THE UNIVERSITY OF MARYLAND. THEY WON THE CASE, AND DONALD GAINES MURRAY (CENTER) BECAME THE FIRST BLACK STUDENT ADMITTED TO THE LAW SCHOOL.

By 1940, Marshall was head of the NAACP Legal Defense and Educational Fund. But he did not get to stay at home in New York. To raise money for the Fund and to work on cases, he traveled 50,000 miles per year.

In his early years with the NAACP, Marshall tried many cases. A number of these were filed to integrate schools. Some of Marshall's cases were for serious crimes, such as murder. Often his clients were innocent. He did not win every case, however. Many white people still believed that all black people were bad. Sometimes innocent people were put to death. Marshall did not believe in the **death penalty.** He believed that death was not a fair punishment for any crime. He knew that black and poor people were given the death penalty more often than anyone else. The death penalty was often a result of racism and **prejudice.** Losing these cases made him work even harder to win.

Marshall believed that all public places in the United States should be integrated. He knew that the best way to make this happen was to focus on one thing first. He decided to concentrate on integrating schools.

AS HEAD OF THE NAACP LEGAL DEFENSE AND EDUCATIONAL FUND, MARSHALL TRAVELED AROUND THE COUNTRY TO HELP PEOPLE.

Marshall became the head lawyer in a 1954 lawsuit known as *Brown versus the Board of Education of Topeka* (Kansas). Reverend Oliver Brown was an African American father in Topeka who sued the school board. His daughter, Linda, had to cross the railroad tracks to get to school. This was too dangerous for a little girl. Reverend Brown wanted Linda to be able to go to the public school closest to their home.

Leaders of the Topeka NAACP asked other African American parents to be part of a case as well. Soon, 13 families agreed to take part in the challenge to end segregation in public schools. The case was brought before the Supreme Court. All nine judges on the Court **ruled** in favor of ending school segregation. They stated, "Does segregation of children in public schools solely on the basis of race … deprive the children of the **minority** group of equal educational opportunities? We believe that it does."

The country was shocked. Such a ruling had never been made before.

African Americans were very happy. Marshall became a hero. *Brown versus the Board of Education of Topeka* (Kansas) was one of the most important court cases in U.S. history. Marshall was so famous that a song was made up about him. It was titled "Thurgood Marshall, Mr. Civil Rights" and was sung to the tune of "The Ballad of Davy Crockett."

Thurgood … Thurgood Marshall,
* Mr. Civil Rights.*
Born in Maryland, the state of the free,
Went to Howard for his law degree,
Took his training at Charlie's knee,
Said, "It isn't so free, as you can see."

Thurgood … Thurgood Marshall,
* Mr. Civil Rights.*
Fought for the teachers, fought for
* the schools,*
Went down south where they broke
* all the rules,*
Now he's working on the swimming pools,
Justice and right are his fighting tools.

Thurgood … Thurgood Marshall,
* Mr. Civil Rights.*

MARSHALL WORKED ON SEVERAL ANTISEGREGATION CASES. IN 1956, HE HELPED AUTHERINE LUCY (SHOWN TO MARSHALL'S LEFT) WIN ADMITTANCE TO THE UNIVERSITY OF ALABAMA. MARSHALL OBTAINED A COURT ORDER FORCING THE UNIVERSITY TO ADMIT THE 26-YEAR-OLD STUDENT.

While Marshall was busy at work on court cases, his wife Buster became sick. She did not want to worry her husband, so she did not tell him how sick she really was. Not long after Marshall won the famous case, Buster told him she had cancer.

Throughout their marriage, Marshall's job had required him to travel most of the time. Sometimes he was gone for weeks. His wife's cancer shocked him. He regretted having spent so much time away from home in the previous years. He had known she was sick but had not known how serious it was. He loved his wife very much. He decided to stay at home to care for her in the last months of her life.

Buster Marshall died on her birthday in 1955. She was 44 years old. The couple had been married for 25 years, and her death left Marshall very sad.

Corbis

IN 1957, THE STUDENTS SHOWN HERE WERE AMONG THE FIRST NINE AFRICAN AMERICANS TO ATTEND CENTRAL HIGH SCHOOL IN LITTLE ROCK, ARKANSAS. WHITE PEOPLE IN THE CITY WERE OUTRAGED AND TRIED TO STOP THEM FROM ATTENDING. THE NEXT YEAR, THE SCHOOL BOARD TOLD THE STUDENTS NOT TO RETURN. MARSHALL ARGUED AGAINST THE SCHOOL BOARD'S EFFORT, AND THE STUDENTS WENT TO WASHINGTON, D.C., TO WATCH THE TRIAL. MARSHALL AND THE STUDENTS POSED FOR THIS PHOTOGRAPH ON THE STEPS OF THE SUPREME COURT BUILDING.

ARTIST NORMAN ROCKWELL CREATED THIS PAINTING DURING THE YEARS IN WHICH AFRICAN AMERICANS STRUGGLED TO END SEGREGATION. IT DEPICTS POLICE ESCORTING A YOUNG BLACK GIRL TO AN ALL-WHITE SCHOOL. ENDING SEGREGATION WAS NOT EASY. AFRICAN AMERICANS FACED ANGER AND VIOLENCE FROM MANY WHITE PEOPLE.

The Supreme Court

Some time after Buster Marshall's death, Marshall began to see a young woman named Cecilia Suyat. She was a secretary at the NAACP. Everyone called her Cissy. She was born in Hawaii, and her parents were from the Philippines. Cissy and Thurgood fell in love and were married. They had two sons. Marshall was pleased, for he had always wanted to have at least one son. The elder boy, Thurgood Jr., was nicknamed "Goody" after his father. The younger son was named John William. For many years, Marshall had worked hard for civil rights. Now he spent time with his new family. He loved to play with his sons and his model trains. For the first time, Marshall took a break from work to enjoy his life.

Marshall was not the only person working for equality in the United States. All across the country, the **Civil Rights Movement** was growing. New leaders, such as the Reverend Martin Luther King Jr., were starting to be noticed.

King was a preacher who worked in Montgomery, Alabama. In December of 1955, an African American woman in Montgomery named Rosa Parks was told to give up her bus seat to a white person. A law required black passengers to sit in the back of buses. It also required them to give up their seats to whites if there were not enough seats for everybody. But Rosa Parks was tired of such inequality. She said no and was arrested.

Black people knew that Rosa Parks's arrest was wrong. If blacks paid the same fare as everyone else, they shouldn't be forced to ride at the back of the bus or to stand. Reverend King urged blacks to start a **protest**—a **boycott** of the public buses. The Montgomery boycott lasted for 382 days. The city did not back down, even though it lost a lot of money from the bus fares. Thurgood Marshall did not believe in protests. He knew they could be dangerous for black people. Instead, he believed in fighting prejudice through the court system.

Library of Congress

MARSHALL MARRIED CECILIA SUYAT IN DECEMBER OF 1955. THEY HAD TWO SONS, AND MARSHALL WAS THRILLED TO BE A FATHER. HE TRIED TO SPEND AS MUCH TIME AS POSSIBLE WITH HIS NEW FAMILY.

Marshall and the NAACP supported Rosa Parks's case and even took it to the Supreme Court. Once again, the NAACP won a case to end segregation. Afterward, Reverend King became the first black man to ride on one of Montgomery's newly integrated buses. He also became famous as a civil rights leader.

Marshall decided that he needed a break from his job. Black leaders in the African country of Kenya invited him to visit their nation. They asked him to help them write a new constitution. Marshall thought that the U.S. Constitution was the best in the world.

He felt that it should apply to everyone, no matter what their color or race. Marshall based Kenya's constitution on the U.S. Constitution. He was proud to help the Kenyan people.

When he returned from Kenya, Marshall learned that students in the South had begun to hold **"sit-ins"** at lunch counters. They wanted to desegregate them. The students would go into a restaurant and sit at the counter. They would ask nicely to be served. When they were told no and asked to leave, they refused to move. Then the police arrested them. The students wanted to be arrested.

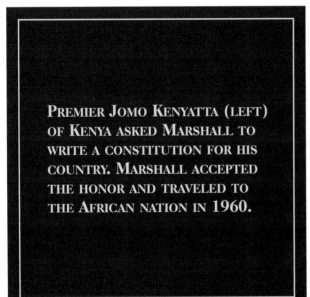

PREMIER JOMO KENYATTA (LEFT) OF KENYA ASKED MARSHALL TO WRITE A CONSTITUTION FOR HIS COUNTRY. MARSHALL ACCEPTED THE HONOR AND TRAVELED TO THE AFRICAN NATION IN 1960.

Library of Congress

The protesters believed they could change the law only by being arrested and going to court. Only by going to court could the law be changed. More than 1,700 students were arrested at sit-ins during the Civil Rights Movement. Marshall still did not approve of protests. He was afraid that they were unsafe and could become violent. But he agreed to defend the students before the Supreme Court. The Court ruled in favor of Marshall and the students, ending segregation in restaurants.

THESE THREE YOUNG MEN PARTICIPATED IN A SIT-IN AT A LUNCH COUNTER IN NORTH CAROLINA. IN THE 1960s, SIT-INS WERE A COMMON FORM OF PROTEST. THURGOOD MARSHALL BELIEVED IT WAS BEST TO FIGHT RACISM BY CHANGING LAWS, NOT BY HOLDING PROTESTS. STILL, HE WENT TO COURT TO HELP A GROUP OF STUDENTS WHO WERE ARRESTED DURING A SIT-IN.

By this time, Marshall was 53 years old. He was known around the world as "Mr. Civil Rights." He was the most famous and important lawyer in the country. Most people who met Marshall liked him. He was fun to be around and had lots of charm. He could talk to anybody and liked to tell good stories. Even some people who were prejudiced against African Americans liked him. Marshall's easy manner helped him win cases. He had worked for the NAACP for 25 years. In that time he had won 29 of the 32 cases he had argued before the U.S. Supreme Court. Judges and other lawyers liked him. Marshall knew when to talk about the law, and he knew when to talk like an ordinary person.

President John F. Kennedy knew that Thurgood Marshall was a good lawyer. In 1961, he offered Marshall a new job as a **federal** judge on the U.S. Second Circuit Court of Appeals in New York City. Marshall became the first African American ever to serve on this court. This was an important job. Sometimes when people go to court, they do not believe the judge has ruled fairly. They can **appeal** their case and have the ruling reviewed by a higher court. As an appeals court judge, Marshall wrote 112 court decisions. The Supreme Court, the highest court in the land, has never overturned or reversed any of those decisions.

Marshall served as a federal judge for several years. Then one day, he received a phone call. President Lyndon Baines Johnson wanted him to be the U.S. **solicitor** general. The job of the solicitor general is to argue the national government's side in cases before the Supreme Court. No African American had ever held such a high-level government job. Marshall was excited about his new job but also a little worried. His job as a judge was for life. He could not be fired or replaced. But if he took the job as solicitor general, the next president could replace him. He would also earn less money. But it was not every day that the president of the United States called to offer a job. Marshall accepted.

Thurgood Marshall was an excellent solicitor general. He won 14 out of the 19 cases he argued before the Supreme Court. In fact, Marshall argued and won more cases before the Supreme Court than anyone else. As solicitor general, he continued to fight discrimination.

Lyndon Baines Johnson Library

MARSHALL (LEFT) IS SHOWN HERE WITH PRESIDENT LYNDON
BAINES JOHNSON, ONE OF HIS GREATEST SUPPORTERS. JOHNSON
FIRST NAMED MARSHALL THE U.S. SOLICITOR GENERAL AND
LATER NAMED HIM A JUSTICE TO THE SUPREME COURT.

President Johnson was pleased with Marshall. The two men got along well and became friends. They were both big, tall men. They were easygoing and liked to share jokes and tell wild stories. But their lives were not all fun and jokes. Both men worked hard for civil rights. Each respected the other. Johnson decided to offer Marshall an even more important position. In 1967, he **appointed** Marshall to the Supreme Court as a **justice**. Nine judges sit on the Supreme Court. Marshall's first words upon hearing the news were "Oh, yipe!" He was very surprised. It was his life-long dream come true. In law school, he used to go to the Supreme Court to hear the cases. From that time on, Marshall had wanted to be a Supreme Court justice. Now it had actually happened.

As a justice, Marshall kept working for civil rights for all Americans. He included poor and homeless people in his fight for civil rights. He also worked for the rights of prisoners. He believed strongly in affirmative action. This meant that the government would "affirm" or say "yes" to giving people in minority groups an equal chance for jobs and education. Marshall knew that all people were not fair in their hearts. Affirmative action made sure that they treated others fairly by law. Minority people were not just black people. They were all people who belonged to a smaller group within the population. Asian and Latin people were minorities. Even women were considered minorities because they often did not have the same opportunities as men. All minorities gained from affirmative action. It gave more Americans an equal start in life.

When Marshall first became a Supreme Court justice, most of the other justices agreed with him on important court decisions. He was a Supreme Court justice for 24 years. During this time, all of the other justices retired or passed away. New presidents appointed new justices. In time, Marshall found that he was in the minority on the Court. Some of the new justices did not believe in affirmative action. Their ideas about civil rights were different from his. The country began to change.

IN 1967, THURGOOD MARSHALL (STANDING AT FAR RIGHT) BECAME ONE OF THE NINE JUSTICES OF THE U.S. SUPREME COURT. HE WAS THE FIRST AFRICAN AMERICAN TO RECEIVE THIS GREAT HONOR.

Thurgood Marshall's Legacy

As Marshall grew older, people recognized his hard work for civil rights. They began to build monuments in his honor and name schools after him. The University of Maryland renamed their law school after Thurgood Marshall. This did not please him. Fifty years earlier, this same school had refused to admit him because he was black. He was still angry that he hadn't been allowed to go there. But to most other people, the renamed law school was a sign of progress. It made many Americans proud to have a school named after a black person.

Marshall posed for a sculptor to make a statue of him. It stands in front of the federal building in his hometown of Baltimore. He also gave all of his notes and papers from his entire career to the Library of Congress. By doing so, he made sure that students could study all of his legal ideas and decisions for years to come.

Marshall served as a Supreme Court justice from October 2, 1967, until October 1, 1991. During that time, he saw many changes in the country and on the Court. Six different presidents held office while Marshall sat on the bench. Marshall had once said that he would serve out his life term as a justice. But times had changed. For a long time, he had been in poor health. He finally **resigned** from the Supreme Court in 1991. President George Bush appointed Clarence Thomas to replace Marshall. Thomas was also an African American, but he did not agree with Marshall's views on equality and civil rights. Thomas did not believe in affirmative action. In fact, he did not think that the *Brown versus the Board of Education of Topeka* (Kansas) decision was correct. Being replaced by Thomas made Marshall unhappy. He did not want all of his hard work to come undone after he retired.

THE SUPREME COURT HAS SAT IN THE COURTROOM SHOWN ABOVE SINCE 1935. THURGOOD MARSHALL WORKED THERE FROM 1967 THROUGH 1991.

Office of the Curator, The Supreme Court of the United States

MARSHALL (SEATED SECOND FROM RIGHT) AND THE OTHER EIGHT SUPREME COURT JUSTICES POSED FOR THIS OFFICIAL PORTRAIT IN NOVEMBER OF 1990, ABOUT ONE YEAR BEFORE MARSHALL RESIGNED FROM HIS POST.

Thurgood Marshall died on January 24, 1993. He was 84 years old. Thousands of people from all over the country went to Washington, D.C., to pay their respects. Many people believe that through his legal work, Marshall did more for equality in the United States than anyone else. He also set a strong example for his sons to follow. His son Thurgood Jr. is a lawyer. Marshall's son John William became a police officer.

At Monroe Elementary School in Topeka, Kansas, is the *Brown versus the Board of Education of Topeka* (Kansas) National Historic Site. It honors the 1954 Supreme Court decision that de-segregated the public schools. Monroe is the school that Oliver Brown had wanted his daughter Linda to attend.

Marshall never called himself an African American. He did not call himself black. He came from an earlier time when people used the words "Negro" and "colored." He used those terms all his life. When he was older, he sometimes used the term "Afro-American." It did not matter what words Marshall used to describe himself. He knew that all men and women are equal. Words could not limit that equality, and he never let words limit him. Look around your neighborhood or school. Are there students there of a different color or race than you? If so, then Thurgood Marshall is one of the reasons why you and your friends of different colors and races can live and learn together.

Office of the Curator, The Supreme Court of the United States

AFTER THURGOOD MARSHALL DIED, A FORMER ASSISTANT WROTE THAT HE "HAD THE CAPACITY TO IMAGINE A RAD-ICALLY DIFFERENT WORLD ... AND THE COURAGE AND ABILITY TO MAKE THAT IMAGINED WORLD REAL."

Corbis

Timeline

1908 — Thoroughgood Marshall is born in Baltimore, Maryland, on July 2. As a little boy, he changes the spelling of his name to "Thurgood."

1926 — Marshall goes to college at Lincoln University in Pennsylvania. He becomes friends with the famous poet Langston Hughes, who teaches him about prejudice.

1929 — Marshall marries Vivian "Buster" Burey.

1930 — Marshall graduates from Lincoln University with honors.

Marshall wants to attend the University of Maryland Law School, but the school does not admit black students. He enrolls at Howard University instead. At Howard, Marshall meets Charles Hamilton Houston, who will become his role model.

1933 — Marshall receives his law degree from Howard University.

1934 — Marshall goes to work for the National Association for the Advancement of Colored People (NAACP). As an NAACP lawyer, he will win many important cases in the next 25 years.

1936 — Marshall argues and wins the case that desegregates the University of Maryland.

1940 — The NAACP names Marshall the head of its Legal Defense and Educational Fund.

1954 — The Supreme Court rules on the case of *Brown versus the Board of Education of Topeka* (Kansas) to end segregation in all public schools. It is the most important case of Marshall's career.

1955 — Following the death of his first wife, Buster, Marshall marries Cecilia "Cissy" Suyat. In December, Rosa Parks is arrested in Montgomery, Alabama, for refusing to give up her bus seat to a white person.

1956 — The Marshalls' first son, Thurgood Jr., is born. Black people in Montgomery boycott the city's buses throughout the year to protest segregation. The NAACP argues the case that desegregates Montgomery's buses.

1958 — Marshall's second son, John William, is born.

1960 — Marshall travels to Kenya to help its government write a constitution. He bases it on the U.S. Constitution, which he believes is the best in the world.

1961 — President Kennedy appoints Marshall to be a federal judge in the Second District Court of Appeals in New York City.

1965 — Marshall becomes the first African American to be appointed U.S. solicitor general. He wins 14 of 19 cases he tries for the government between 1965 and 1967.

1967 — Marshall becomes the first African American appointed to the U.S. Supreme Court. He continues his work to guarantee civil rights to all Americans.

1991 — In poor health, Thurgood Marshall retires from the Supreme Court after 24 years of service. Clarence Thomas is named as his replacement.

1992 — President George Bush names Monroe Elementary School in Topeka, Kansas, a National Historic Site. Plans are underway to create a memorial there for the Supreme Court's *Brown versus the Board of Education of Topeka* (Kansas) decision that desegregated all public schools.

1993 — Thurgood Marshall dies at age 84. Thousands of people mourn his death and the passing of an important civil rights leader.

Glossary

appeal (uh-PEEL)
In law, to appeal is to ask a higher court to review a judge's ruling on a case. Thurgood Marshall's first appointment as a judge was in a court of appeals.

appointed (uh-POYNT-ed)
When someone is appointed to a position, he or she is officially chosen and asked to accept. President Johnson appointed Marshall to be a Supreme Court justice.

boycott (BOY-kot)
A boycott is a protest in which people stop using a certain product or service. A boycott helped end segregation on public buses in the city of Montgomery, Alabama.

cases (KAY-sez)
Cases are matters for a court of law to decide. As a law student, Thurgood Marshall would go to the Supreme Court and listen to lawyers present their cases.

civil rights (SIV-el RYTZ)
Civil rights are a person's rights to freedom and equal treatment. Marshall believed that Americans of all races should be guaranteed civil rights.

Civil Rights Movement (SIV-il RYTZ MOOV-ment)
The Civil Rights Movement was the struggle for equal rights for African Americans in the United States during the 1950s and 1960s. Martin Luther King Jr. was a leader in the Civil Rights Movement.

Constitution (kon-stih-TOO-shun)
A constitution is a document that lays out how a nation's government and laws will work. Thurgood Marshall read and studied the U.S. Constitution in high school.

dean (DEEN)
A dean is the head of a college or school at a university. Charles Hamilton Houston was dean of the law school when Marshall attended Howard University.

death penalty (DETH PEN-ull-tee)
When people receive the death penalty, they are sentenced to die as punishment for their crimes. Marshall believed that the death penalty was wrong.

Glossary

debate (deh-BAYT)
A debate is a discussion between people with different opinions on a subject. William Marshall liked to debate with his sons at dinner.

federal (FED-er-rull)
Federal means having to do with the nation's central government, rather than a state or city government. President Kennedy appointed Marshall to be a federal judge.

Great Depression (GRATE dee-PRESH-un)
The Great Depression was a period during the 1930s in which there was little business activity in the United States, and many people could not find work. Thurgood Marshall opened his law office during the Great Depression and often helped people for free.

integration (in-teh-GRAY-shun)
Integration means bringing together people who had been kept separate, especially because of race. The court decision called *Brown versus the Board of Education of Topeka* (Kansas) led to the integration of public schools.

justice (JUSS-tiss)
A justice is a judge. Thurgood Marshall was one of the nine justices on the U.S. Supreme Court.

minority (mih-NOR-ih-tee)
A minority is a smaller or less powerful group within a larger society, often of a different race or religion. The U.S. Supreme Court decided that children from minority groups should have equal access to education.

minstrel (MIN-strel)
A minstrel is a performer who sings and dances to entertain people. Jim Crow was a black character in a minstrel show.

prejudice (PREH-juh-diss)
Prejudice is a negative feeling or opinion about someone without a good reason. Marshall believed in using the court system to fight prejudice and unequal treatment.

protest (PROH-test)
A protest is a public statement or gathering in which people speak out to say something is wrong. During the Civil Rights Movement, Americans attended protests to speak out against the poor treatment of minorities.

racism (RAY-sih-zim)
Racism is a negative feeling or opinion about people because of their race. Norma and William Marshall tried to protect their sons from racism.

Glossary

resigned (re-ZYND)
When a person has resigned, he or she has left a job or position by choice. In 1991, Thurgood Marshall resigned after serving on the Supreme Court for 24 years.

rule (ROOL)
When a court rules on a case, it makes a decision. In 1954, all nine judges on the Supreme Court ruled to end segregation in public schools.

segregated (SEG-reh-gay-ted)
If people or things are segregated, they are kept apart. Many places in the United States were once segregated, so that African Americans could not enter areas or were kept separate from white people.

sit-ins (SIT-inz)
A sit-in is a kind of protest in which people sit down and refuse to leave. During the Civil Rights Movement, sit-ins helped end segregation in restaurants.

solicitor (suh-LISS-ih-tur)
A solicitor is a lawyer in a city, state, or national government. As U.S. solicitor general, Marshall argued the national government's side in cases before the Supreme Court.

sue (SOO)
When people sue other people, they take them to court to resolve a disagreement. When an African American man sued the University of Maryland in 1936, Thurgood Marshall was one of his lawyers.

Supreme Court (suh-PREEM KORT)
The Supreme Court is the highest court in the United States. Thurgood Marshall was a member of the Supreme Court.

Index

Further Information

Books

Adler, David A., and Robert Casilla. *Picture Book of Thurgood Marshall.* New York: Holiday House, 1999.

Aldred, Lisa. *Thurgood Marshall* (Black Americans of Achievement). Broomall, PA: Chelsea House Publishing, 1990.

Calabro, Marian. *Great Courtroom Lawyers Fighting the Cases That Made History.* New York: Facts on File, 1996.

Kent, Deborah. *Thurgood Marshall and the Supreme Court* (Cornerstones of Freedom). Chicago: Childrens Press, 1997.

Whitelaw, Nancy. *Mr. Civil Rights: The Story of Thurgood Marshall* (Notable Americans). Greensboro, NC: Morgan Reynolds, 1995.

Web Sites

Read some of Thurgood Marshall's speeches and interviews:
http://www.thurgoodmarshall.com/

Visit the African American Odyssey: A Quest for Full Citizenship, at the Library of Congress's Web site:
http://lcweb2.loc.gov/ammem/aaohtml/exhibit/aointro.html

Read the U.S. Constitution:
http://www.house.gov/Constitution/Constitution.html

Visit the Web site of the National Association for the Advancement of Colored People:
http://www.naacp.org/default.asp

Visit the Web site of the United States Supreme Court:
http://www.supremecourtus.gov/

Learn more about *Brown versus the Board of Education of Topeka* (Kansas) at the Brown Foundation for Educational Equity, Excellence and Research:
http://brownvboard.org/

Learn more about Lincoln University, the first historically black university in the U. S.:
http://www.lincoln.edu/president/index.html